learn to draw
Cars, Planes & Moving Machines

Step-by-step instructions for more than 25 high-powered vehicles

ILLUSTRATED BY TOM LAPADULA AND JEFF SHELLY

This library edition published in 2016 by Walter Foster Jr.,
an imprint of Quarto Publishing Group USA Inc.
6 Orchard Road, Suite 100
Lake Forest, CA 92630

Distributed in the United States and Canada by
Lerner Publisher Services
241 First Avenue North
Minneapolis, MN 55401 U.S.A.
www.lernerbooks.com

First Library Edition

Library of Congress Cataloging-in-Publication Data

Learn to draw cars, planes & moving machines : step-by-step instructions for more than 25 high-powered
vehicles / illustrated by Tom La Padula and Jeff Shelly. -- First Library Edition.
     pages cm
  ISBN 978-1-939581-69-3
1. Motor vehicles in art--Juvenile literature. 2. Drawing--Technique--Juvenile literature. 3. Vehicles, Military, in art--Juvenile literature. I. LaPadula, Tom, illustrator. II. Shelly, Jeff, illustrator.
  NC825.A8L435 2016
  743'.8962--dc23
                                                                                    2015008805

012016
1765

9 8 7 6 5 4 3 2 1

Table of Contents

Tools & Materials

There's more than one way to bring moving machines to life on paper—you can use crayons, markers, colored pencils, or even paints. Just be sure you have plenty of good vehicle colors—yellows, reds, grays, and browns.

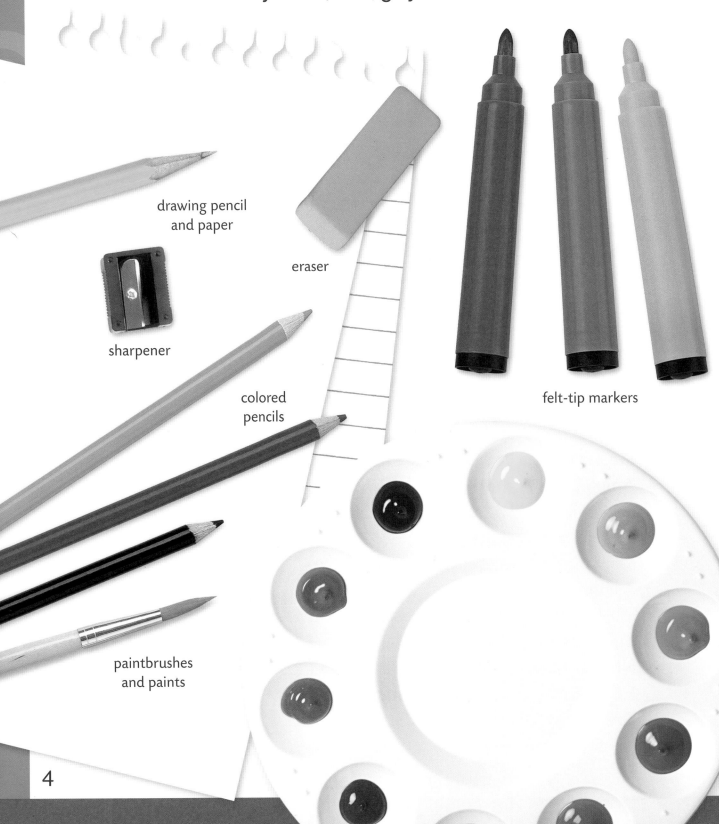

drawing pencil and paper

eraser

sharpener

colored pencils

felt-tip markers

paintbrushes and paints

How to Use This Book

The drawings in this book are made up of basic shapes, such as circles, triangles, and rectangles. Practice drawing the shapes below.

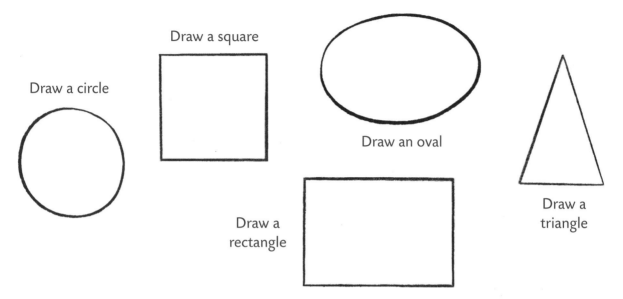

Draw a circle

Draw a square

Draw an oval

Draw a triangle

Draw a rectangle

Notice how these drawings begin with basic shapes.

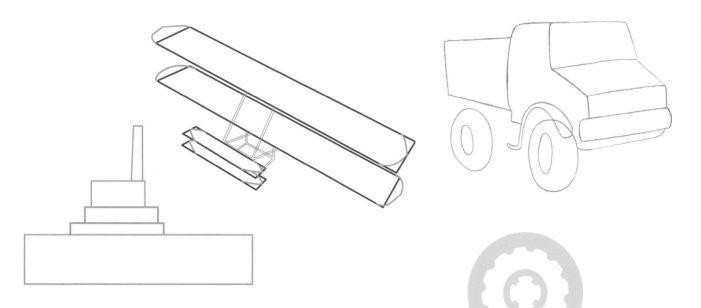

In this book, you'll learn about each featured high-powered vehicle. Look for mini quizzes along the way to learn new and interesting facts!

Look for this symbol, and check your answers on page 64!

Fast, Powerful Moving Machines

In this book you will learn to draw a variety of vehicles.
Below are the main types you will learn about!

Aircraft

These machines are designed to fly through the air and are used for commercial and military purposes. There are two types of aircraft: lighter-than-air, which are supported by their own buoyancy, and heavier-than-air, which require an engine to propel them.

Trucks

These vehicles vary greatly in size, power, and design and are built to carry cargo.

Cars

These vehicles have four wheels and an engine system. Various styles exist, such as the sedan, hatchback, station wagon, and van.

Military Machines

These heavy-duty machines include tanks, armored carriers, 4-, 6-, and 8-wheeled vehicles, military trucks, aircraft, etc. These combat vehicles are designed to be resilient and navigate through trenches and obstacles.

Car History

Below are some quick facts about the history of cars.

The first car made on an assembly line was the Model T Ford. A whopping 15 million were produced between 1908 and 1927!

The world's first automobile was made in France in 1871 by Nicolas Cugnot. Powered by a two-cylinder engine, its top speed was 2.3 mph—walking speed is 3 mph!

In the early 1930s, laws were passed against the first car radios because they were thought to be a distraction to drivers.

Twin-Engine Aircraft

Did You Know?

Twin-engine planes are safer than single-engine planes because they can still fly in the event that one engine fails.

Fun Fact!

This airplane can land on tundras in Alaska or in the wild Australian outback. Special equipment allows the plane to land in remote areas while carrying up to 2,000 pounds of cargo!

This sleek, angular aircraft sports six seats and wingtip-mounted fuel tanks.

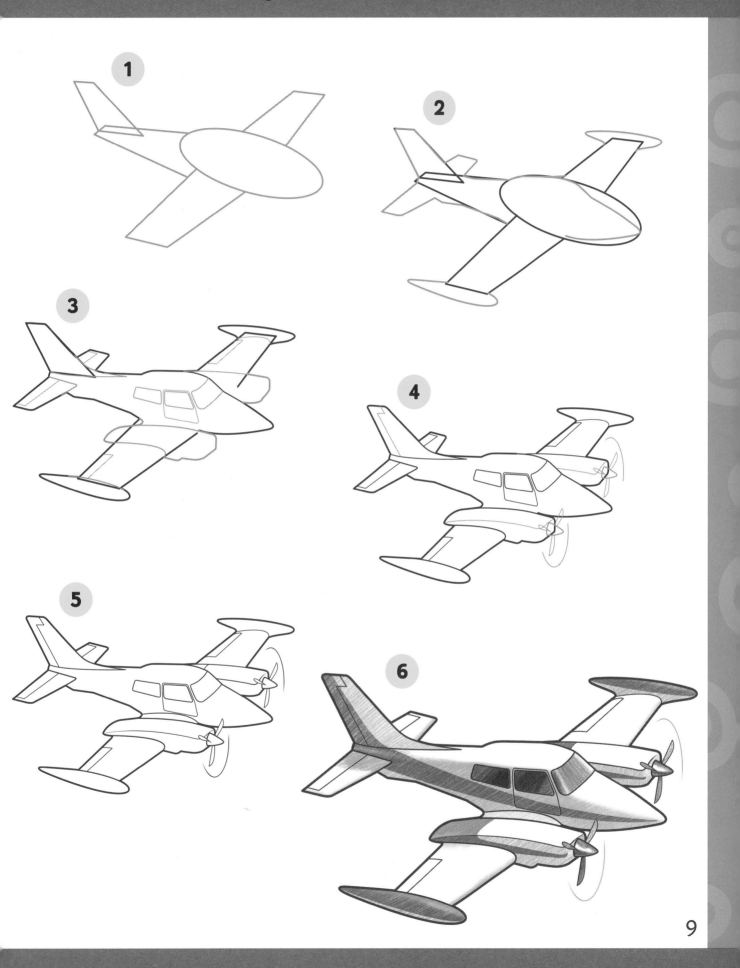

Tandem-Rotor Helicopter

A major advantage of tandem-rotor helicopters is that all of the power produced by the engine is used for lift, while single-rotor helicopters use part of the power to counter the torque.

Did You Know?

Tandem-rotor helicopters are mainly used for large cargo and contain two large horizontal rotors, one in front of the other.

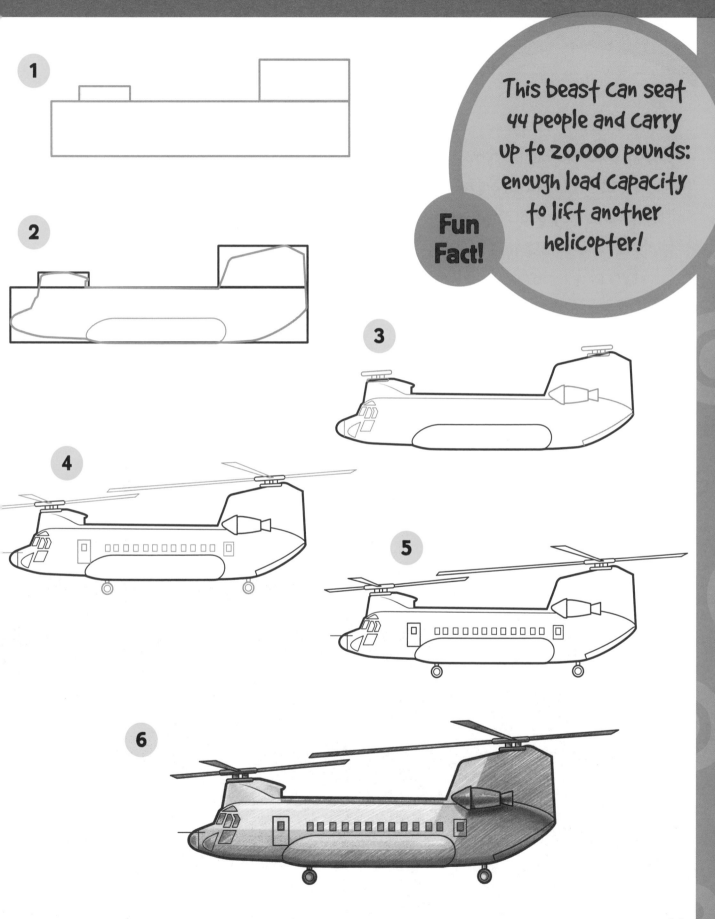

This beast can seat 44 people and carry up to 20,000 pounds: enough load capacity to lift another helicopter!

Fun Fact!

Cargo Ship

Giant cranes move the containers on and off the ships; then they place them onto trains and semitrucks to travel to their final destinations.

Did You Know?

Powered by a diesel engine, this massive vessel transports cargo to shipping ports all over the world.

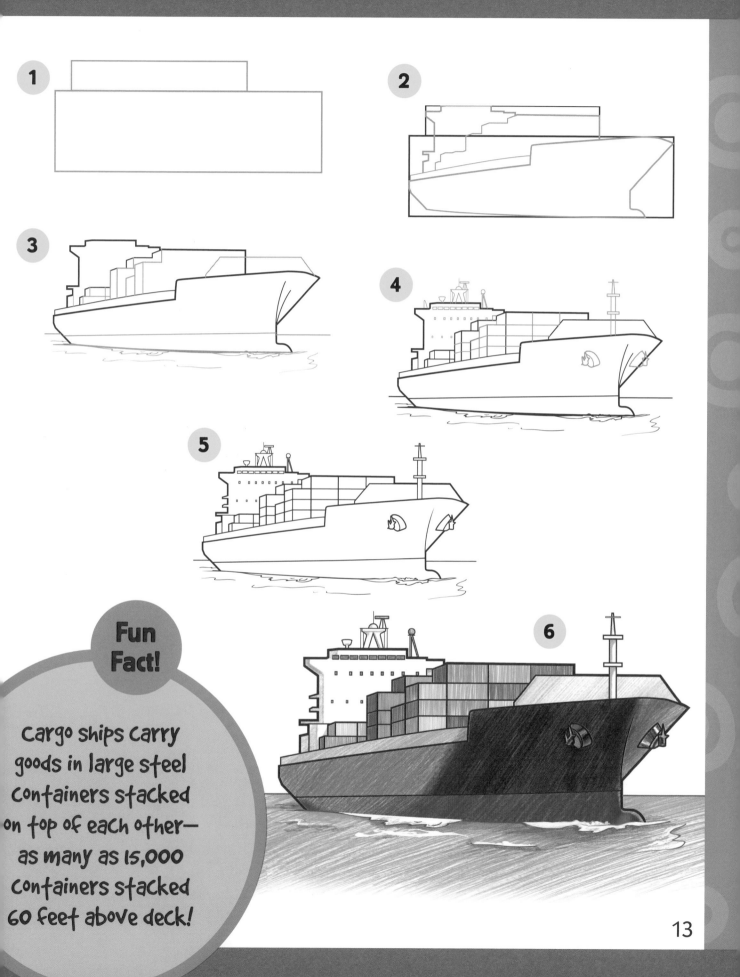

Fun Fact!

cargo ships carry goods in large steel containers stacked on top of each other— as many as 15,000 containers stacked 60 feet above deck!

Three-Engine Wide-Body Aircraft

Did You Know?

This airplane could seat 380 people and fly up to 610 miles per hour.

The three-engine wide-body aircraft was only manufactured from 1971 to 1989.

Mini Quiz

True or false: This aircraft now operates as a cargo plane.

(Answer on page 64)

1

2

3

4

5

6

15

Did You Know?

one of the earliest SAR missions took place in 1656 following the wreck of a Dutch merchant ship off the coast of Australia.

This chopper sports a watertight hull, allowing it to land on water. It's frequently used to rescue people at sea.

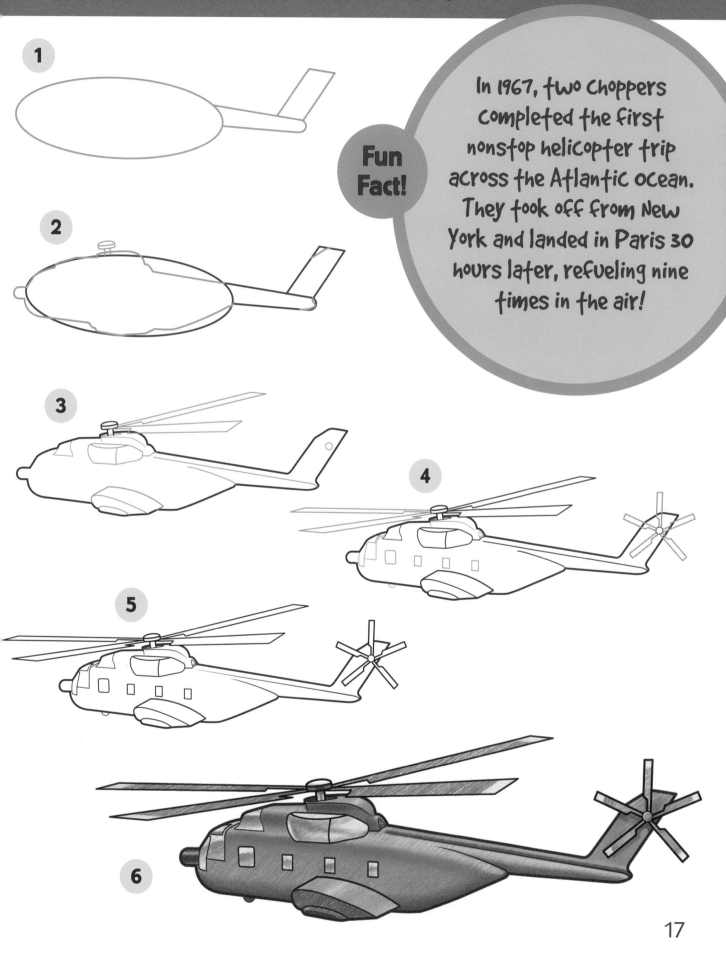

1

2

Fun Fact!

In 1967, two choppers completed the first nonstop helicopter trip across the Atlantic ocean. They took off from New York and landed in Paris 30 hours later, refueling nine times in the air!

3

4

5

6

Tugboat

Fun Fact!

Many tugboats have firefighting monitors, which allow them to assist in firefighting, especially in harbors.

This tough little boat packs a lot of power. It can push or pull cargo ships in and out of crowded canals.

Mini Quiz

How many different types of tugboats are there?

A. 1
B. 2
C. 3
D. 4

(Answer on page 64)

Supersonic Airliner

Did You Know?

Triangular wings and turbo engines help the supersonic airliner travel twice the speed of most other planes.

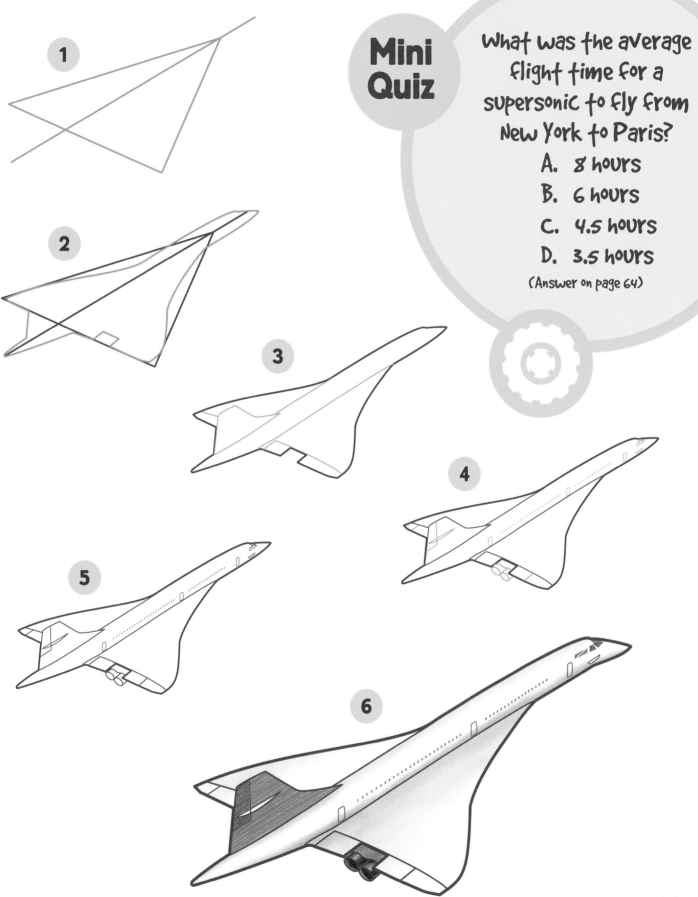

Mini Quiz

What was the average flight time for a supersonic to fly from New York to Paris?
- A. 8 hours
- B. 6 hours
- C. 4.5 hours
- D. 3.5 hours

(Answer on page 64)

Did You Know?

Riverboats have a flat bottom to help steer in shallow water.

This boat uses steam power and large paddles to operate.

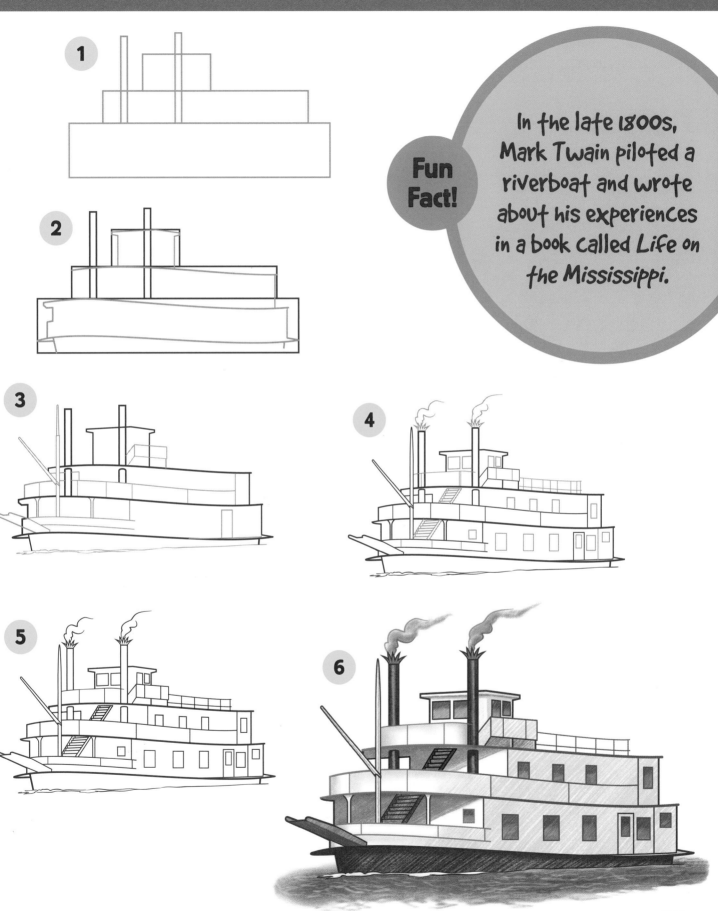

Fun Fact!

In the late 1800s, Mark Twain piloted a riverboat and wrote about his experiences in a book called *Life on the Mississippi.*

23

Light Aerobatic Biplane

Fun Fact!

This plane can perform tricks, including spinning in a roll, looping in a figure eight, and flying upside down!

Did You Know?

Since 1944, this double-winged plane has won hundreds of aerobatic competitions around the world.

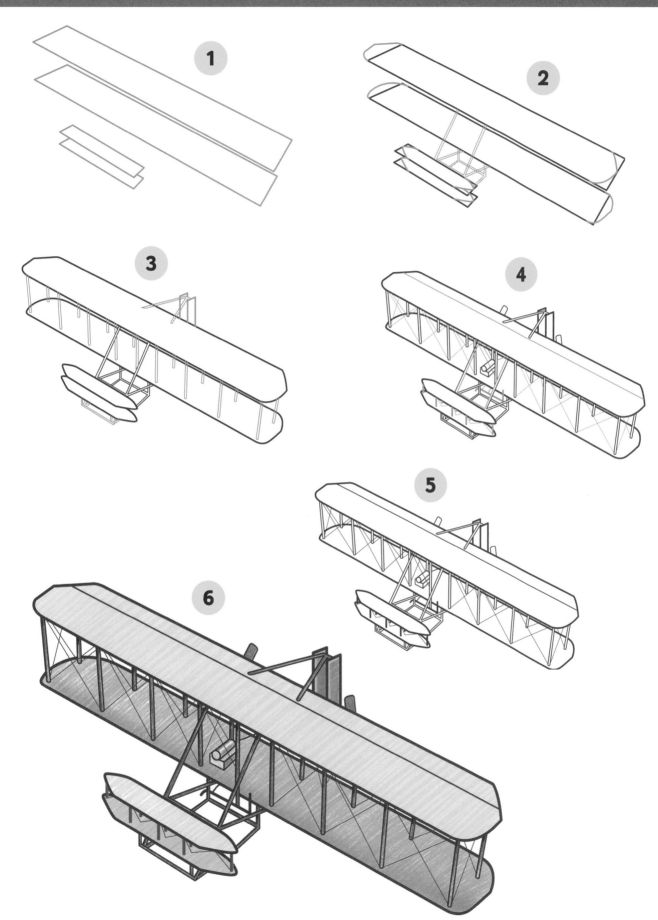

Hovercraft

A hovercraft uses high-speed fans to create an air cushion underneath its rubber sides—it literally floats on air!

Did You Know?

Fun Fact!

Hovercrafts can easily float over mud, so they are often used in rescue operations to help people in flooded areas.

This rectangular craft can jet across ice, snow, and water.

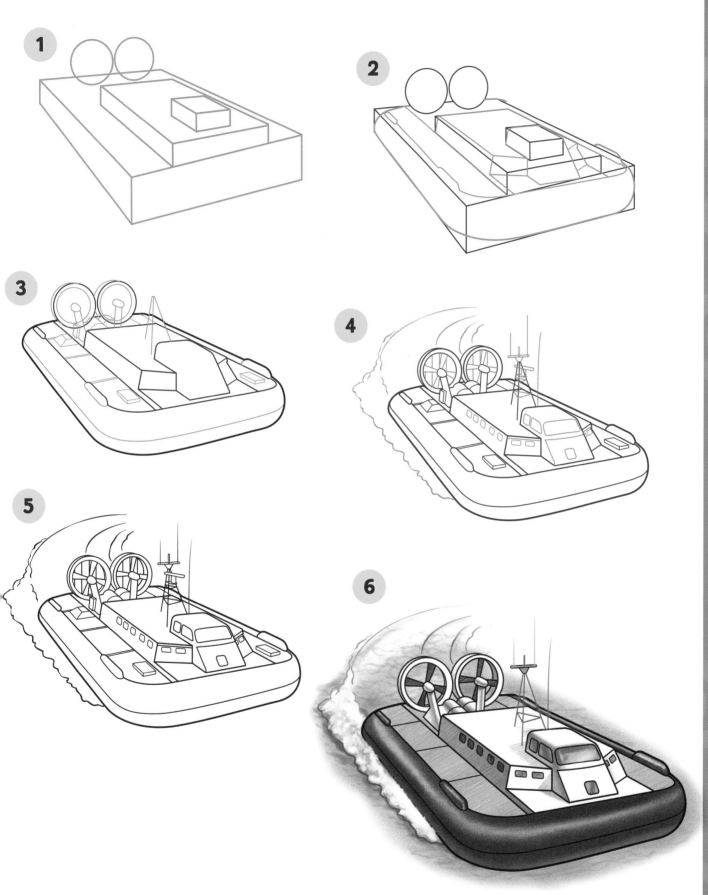

Polar Research Vessel

Its steel hull acts like a sledgehammer, floating up onto ice and crushing it with a 13,000-ton weight.

Fun Fact!

Did You Know?

Early polar research vessels were built of wood with bands of iron wrapped around their hulls to break ice. Modern versions run on multiple gas and diesel-electric engines, and some even use nuclear reactors!

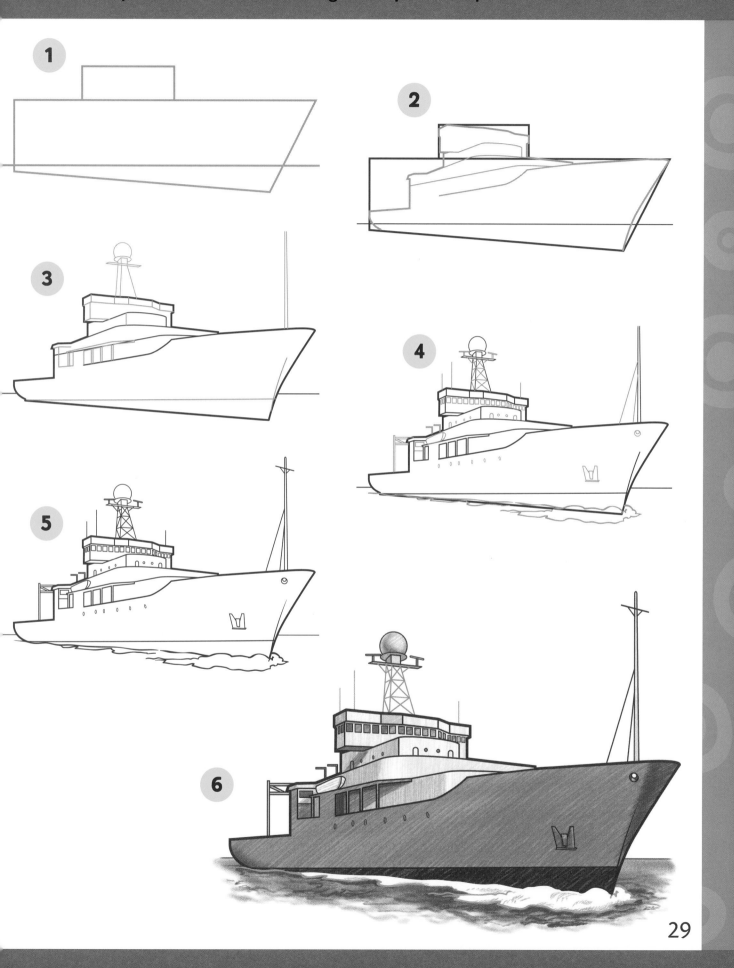

Did You Know?

Steamships were preceded by steamboats, which were propelled by paddlewheels instead of screw propellers and could not travel long distances.

This huge ship runs on steam. Wood or coal burns inside furnaces, heating large boilers filled with water, which produce steam that moves the engines.

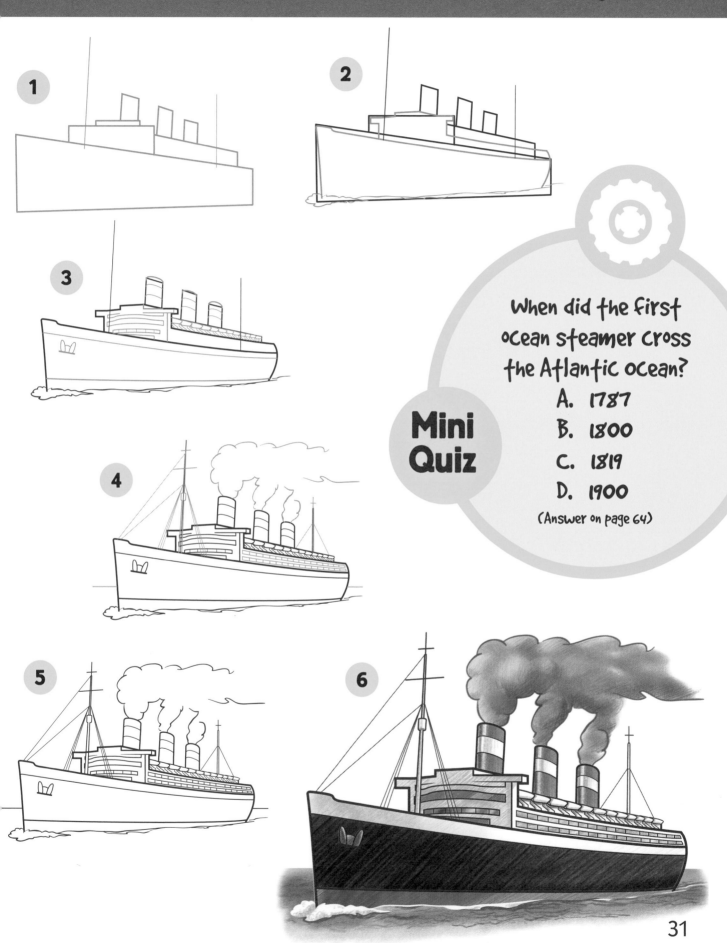

1

2

3

4

5

6

Mini Quiz

When did the first ocean steamer cross the Atlantic ocean?

A. 1787
B. 1800
C. 1819
D. 1900

(Answer on page 64)

Did You Know?

STOL airplanes have a short ground run and can clear obstacles, such as trees, on both takeoff and landing.

First manufactured in 1951, this plane is capable of
landing on both snow and water.

Fun Fact!

This aircraft is sometimes called the "otter" or "King Beaver." Early versions of this easy-to-maneuver plane helped explorers map the Antarctic and Alaska!

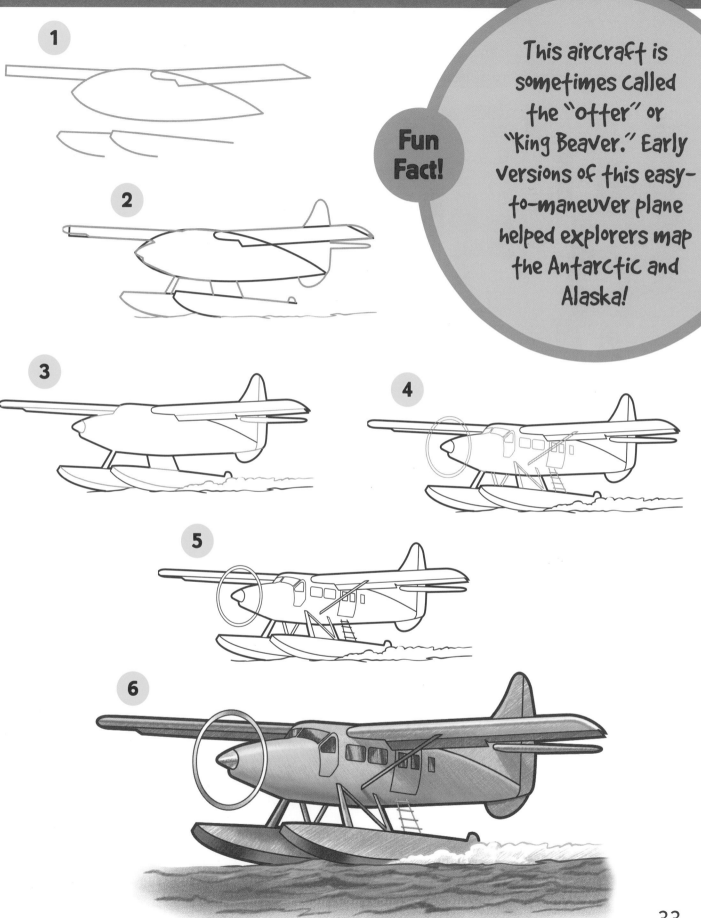

1

2

3

4

5

6

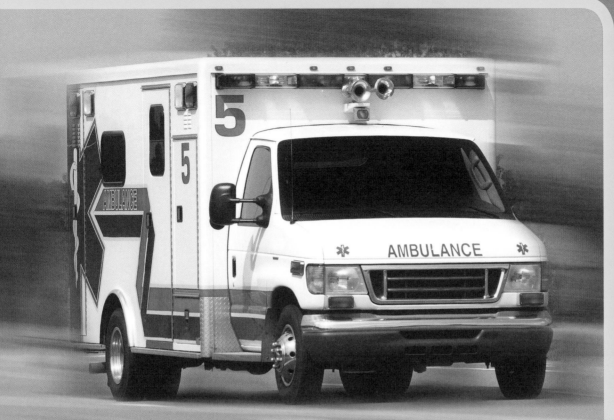

Did You Know?

The word ambulance comes from the Latin word ambulare, meaning "to walk or move about."

This emergency vehicle uses bright colors and a loud siren to clear the way when driving down the road.

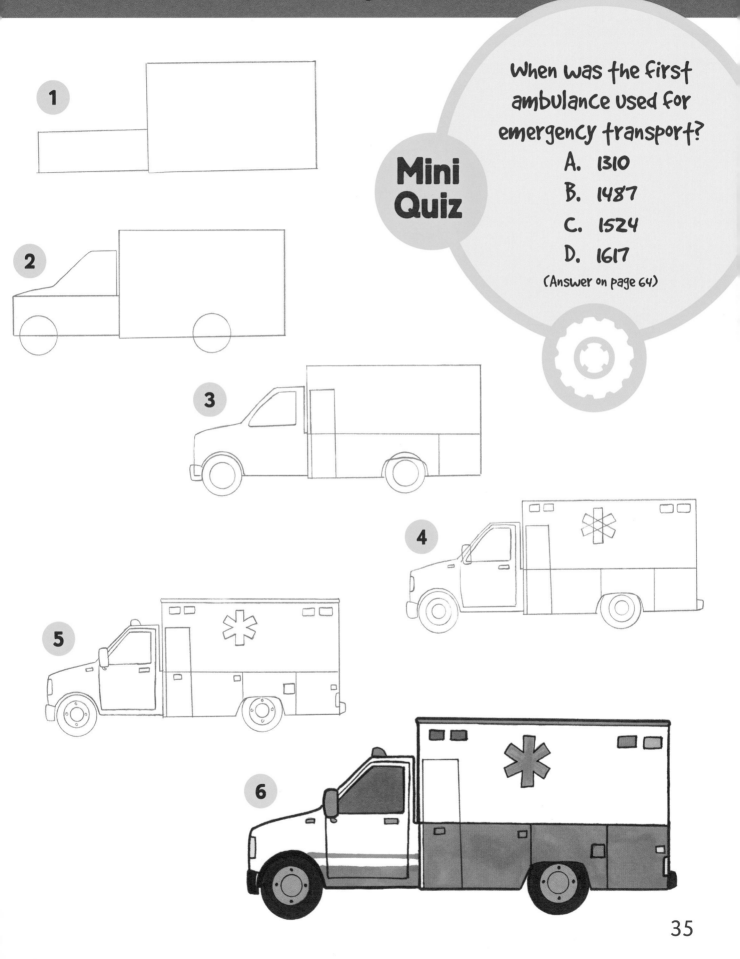

Mini Quiz

When was the first ambulance used for emergency transport?

A. 1310
B. 1487
C. 1524
D. 1617

(Answer on page 64)

1

2

3

4

5

6

Did You Know?

There are almost 20 variants of the HMMWV in service with the United States Armed Forces.

Before it became a consumer sport-utility vehicle, this diesel-fueled machine was used for military purposes.

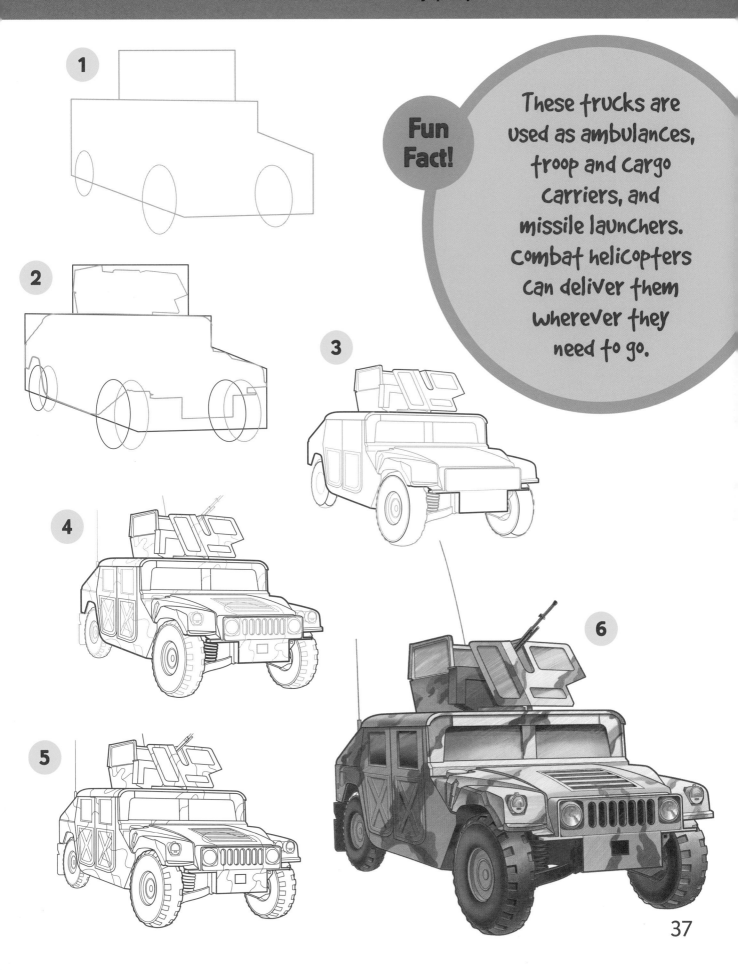

Fun Fact!

These trucks are used as ambulances, troop and cargo carriers, and missile launchers. Combat helicopters can deliver them wherever they need to go.

Dump Truck

The first small dump trucks appeared in the early 1900s. Over time, dump trucks have become so large and powerful that they can carry loads as heavy as a large house!

Fun Fact!

Did You Know?

Most dump trucks today use hydraulics, which refers to the use of an incompressible fluid in the engine, such as oil or water.

This powerful vehicle has a solid frame, very large wheels, and a broad, deep bed that holds heavy loads.

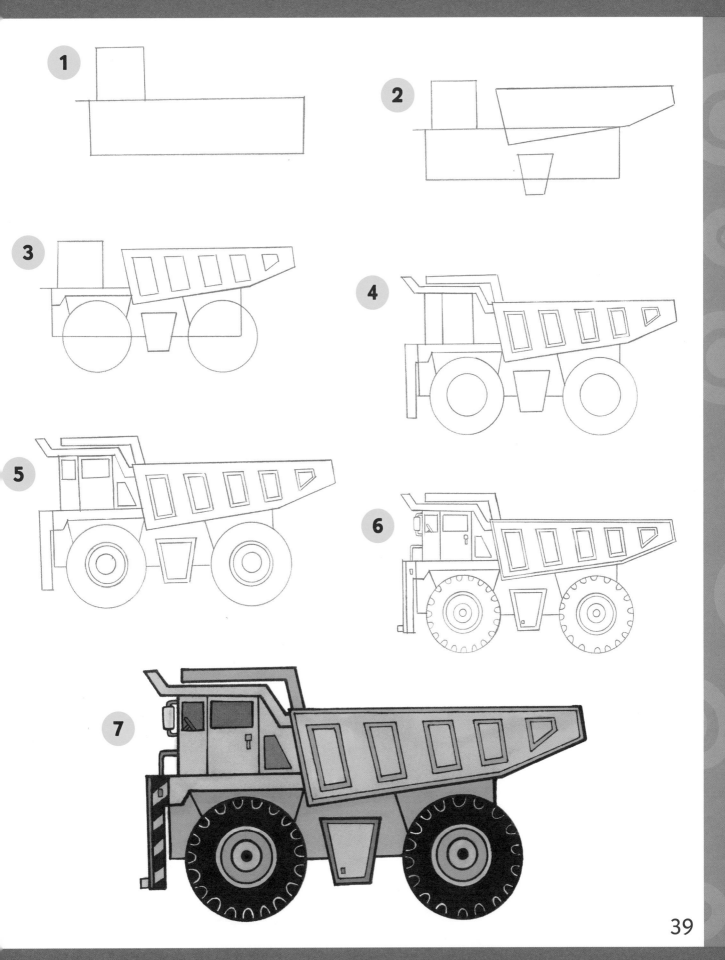

Monster Truck

Did You Know?

These huge trucks are used for competition and entertainment in monster truck shows.

This tall truck has giant wheels that allow it to crawl over giant obstacles—including piles of other cars!

Fun Fact!

The enormous tires used to create monster trucks are usually more than 5 feet tall and 3 feet wide!

1

2

3

4

5

6

Did You Know?

During World War I, the Germans experimented with an early version of a stealth fighter jet.

This sneak-attack jet may look bizarre, but its triangular shape helps it escape radar detection.

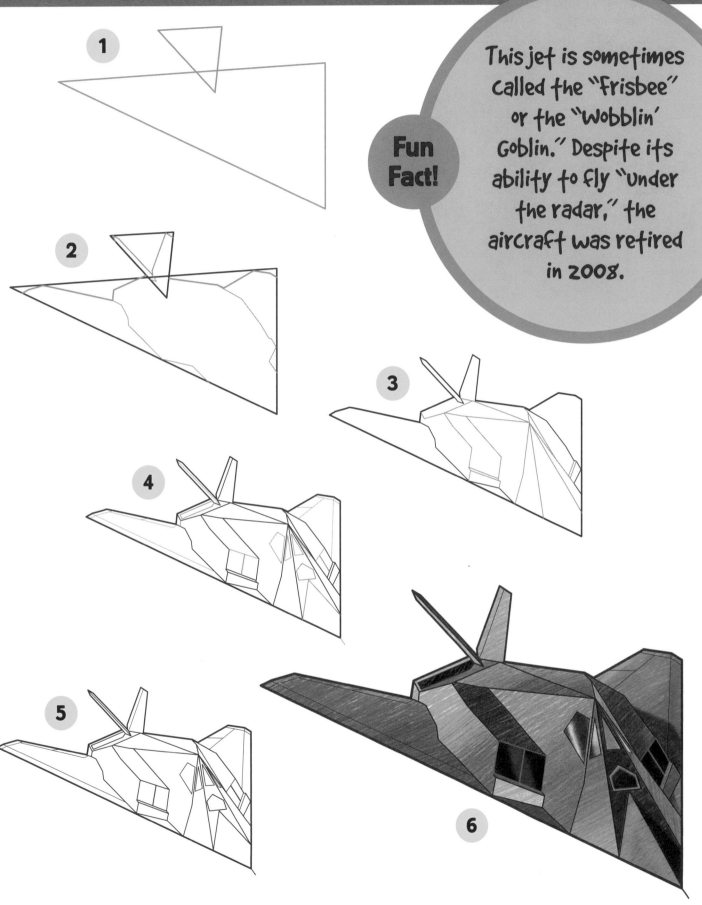

Fun Fact!

This jet is sometimes called the "Frisbee" or the "Wobblin' Goblin." Despite its ability to fly "under the radar," the aircraft was retired in 2008.

Amphibious Armored Car

Did You Know?

This car is "amphibious" because it can travel across both rivers and battlefields with ease.

This multipurpose vehicle is used as an ambulance, anti-tank vehicle, and troop carrier.

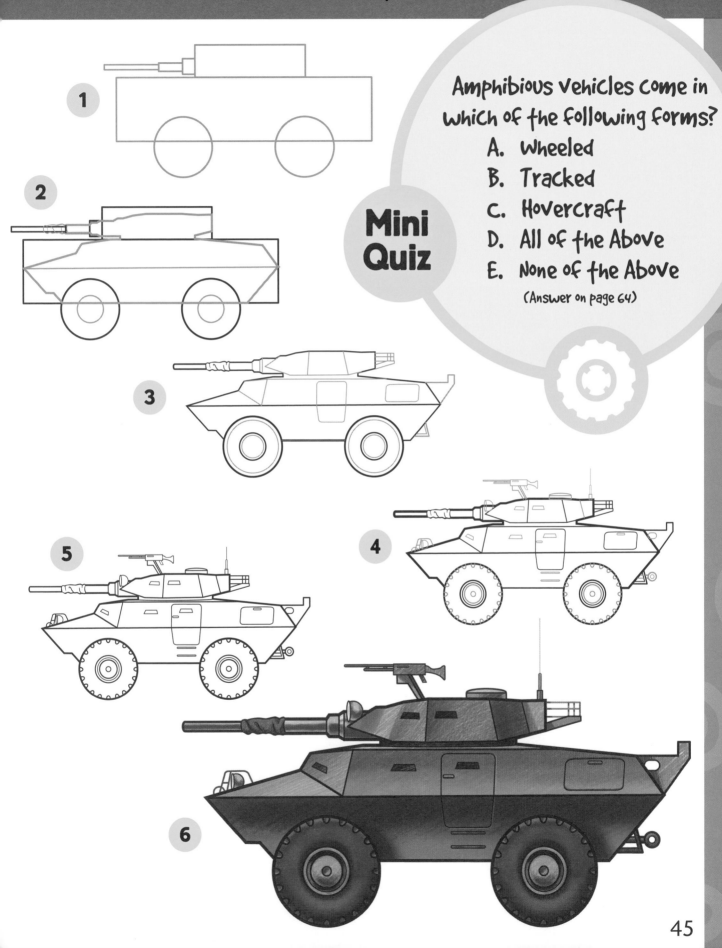

Mini Quiz

Amphibious vehicles come in which of the following forms?
A. Wheeled
B. Tracked
C. Hovercraft
D. All of the Above
E. None of the Above

(Answer on page 64)

45

School Bus

Did You Know?

All school buses have been painted yellow since 1939 when representatives from all 48 states agreed it was easiest to see black lettering against yellow.

The long body of this yellow "limousine" allows for plenty of seats—
some buses can carry more than 80 kids at a time!

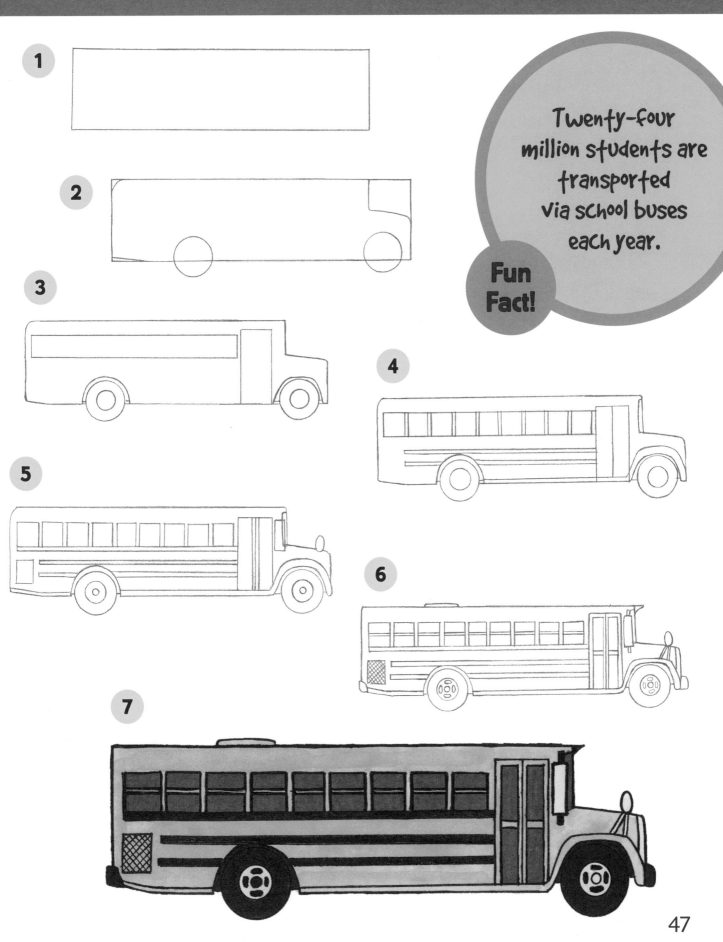

1

2

3

4

5

6

7

Twenty-four million students are transported via school buses each year.

Fun Fact!

Did You Know?

At the touch of a button, the pilot can change the angle of the wings to make it fly faster or slower.

This fighter jet can carry up to 13,000 pounds of missiles.

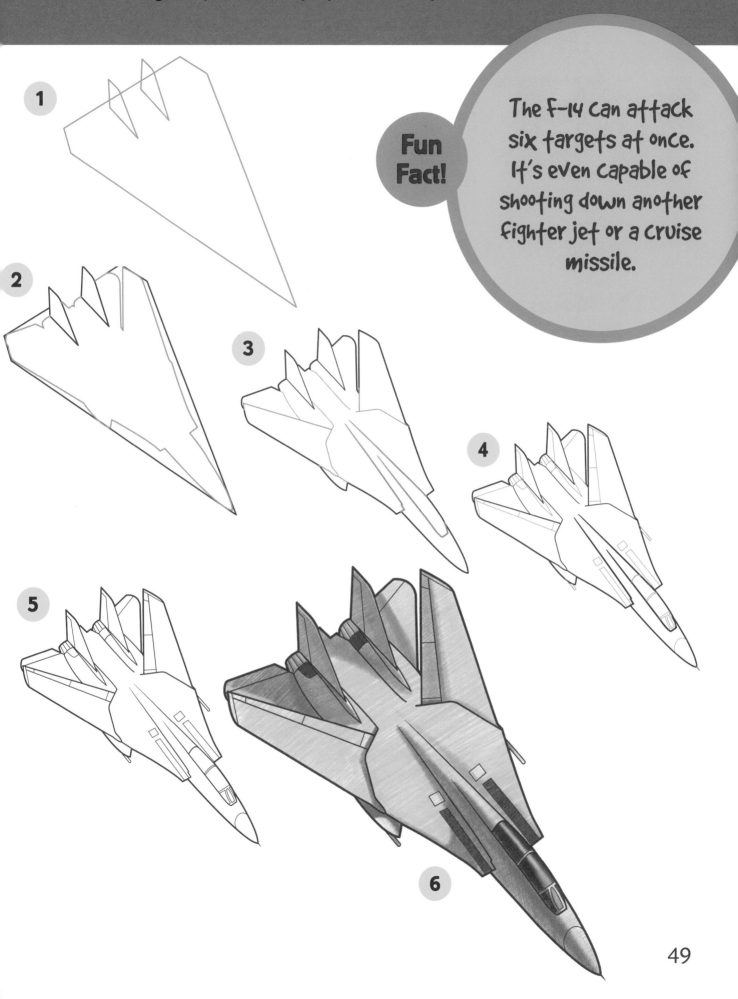

Fun Fact!

The F-14 can attack six targets at once. It's even capable of shooting down another fighter jet or a cruise missile.

1

2

3

4

5

6

Snowplow

Did You Know?

The first snowplow built to be used with motor equipment was in 1913.

This helpful truck has a scoop attached to the front that pushes snow from its path, clearing the streets faster than you can shovel!

Before engines, large wedge-shaped snowplows made of wood were pulled through the streets by horses.

Fun Fact!

Did You Know?

This strong and sturdy vehicle is also known as a "safe on wheels."

This vehicle transports valuables, such as large quantities of money for banks and retail companies.

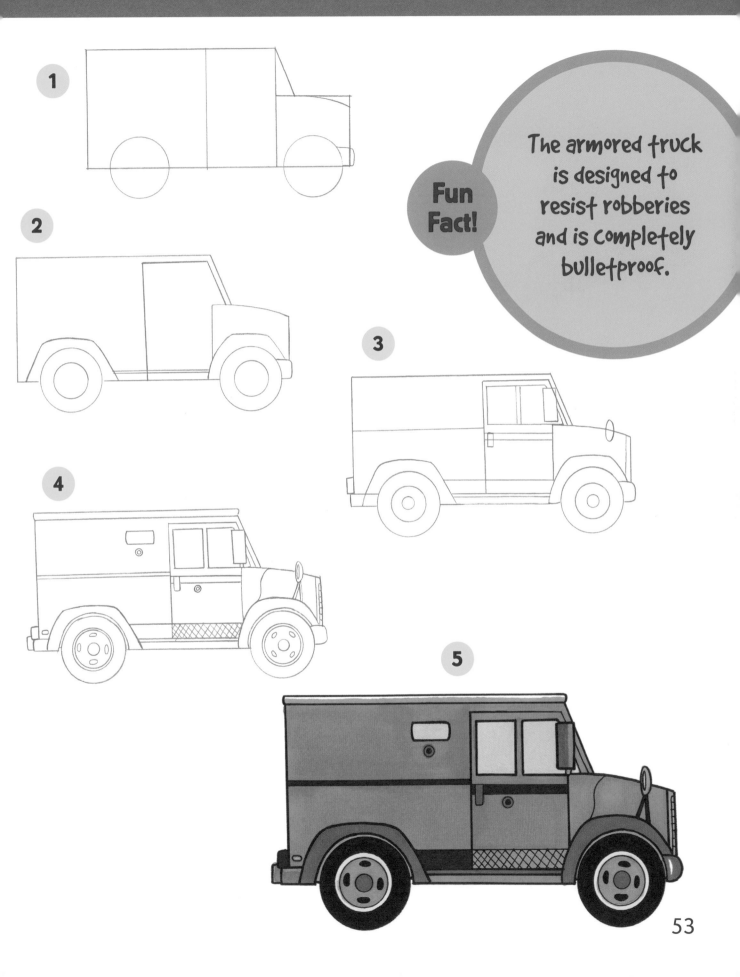

Fun Fact!

The armored truck is designed to resist robberies and is completely bulletproof.

1

2

3

4

5

Tilt-Rotor Aircraft

Did You Know?

Like a helicopter, this aircraft can carry up to 15,000 pounds of cargo on two external hooks, and it can take off and land without a runway. Like a plane, it's able to cruise 30,000 feet above sea level for more than 2,000 miles without refueling!

This bulky gray airplane is able to take off and land vertically and on short runways.

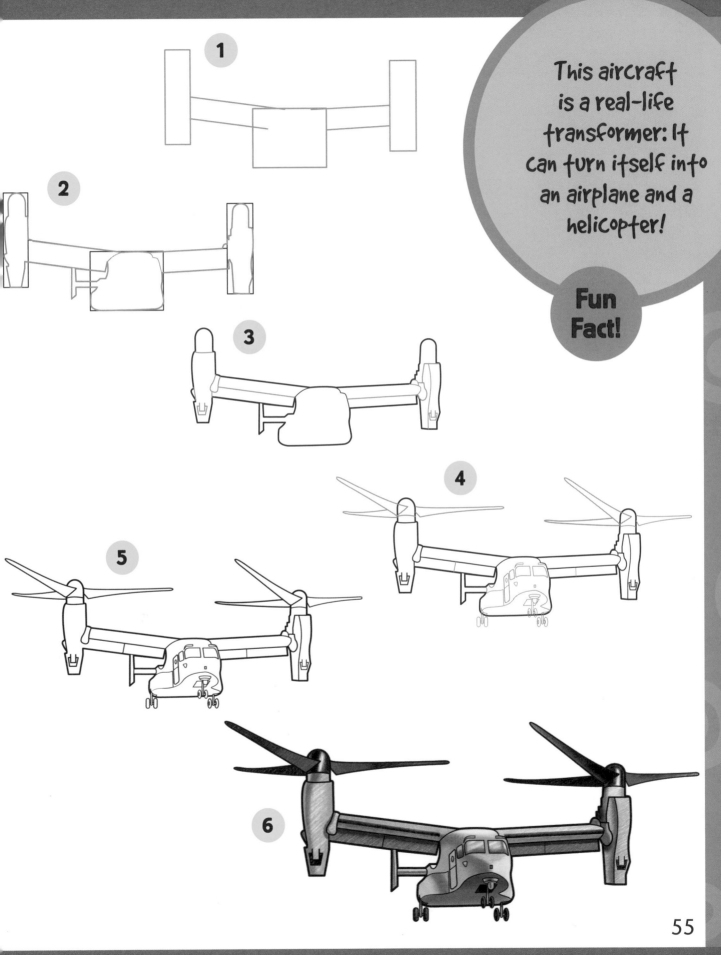

This aircraft is a real-life transformer: It can turn itself into an airplane and a helicopter!

Fun Fact!

Maritime Patrol Aircraft

Did You Know?

The maritime patrol aircraft is often used for search and rescue missions.

This fixed-wing aircraft is designed to operate over water for long durations.

The first maritime patrol aircraft were flown by the Royal Naval Air Service during World War I on anti-submarine patrols.

Fun Fact!

Nuclear-Powered Supercarrier

Did You Know?

The flat deck of this vessel serves as a giant runway.

This enormous ship is used as a portable flight deck for up to 85 airplanes.

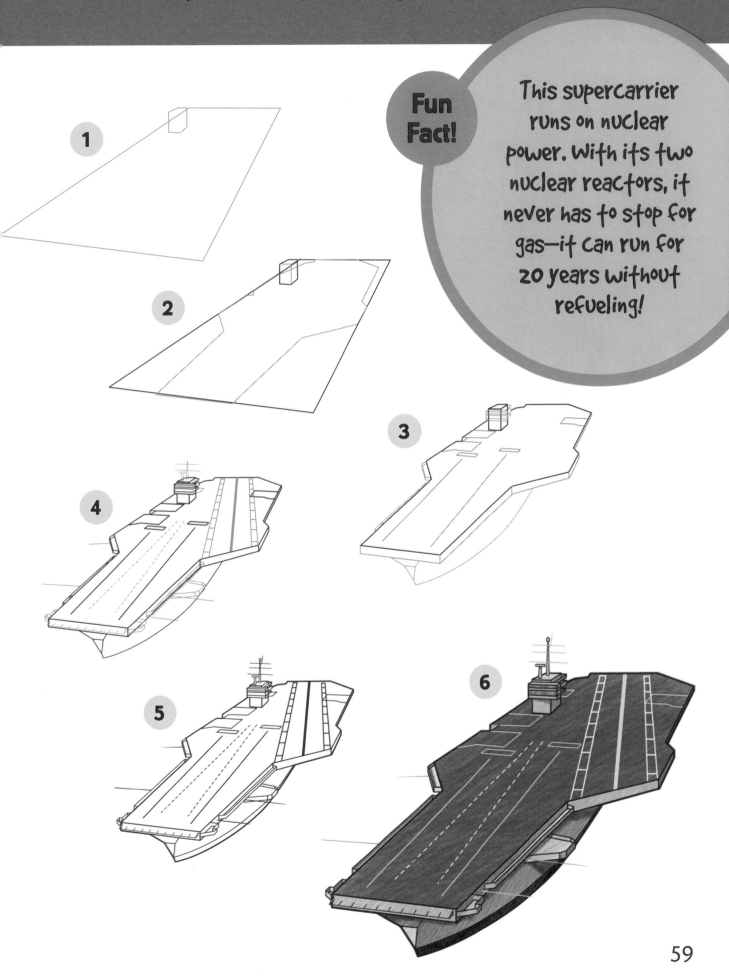

Fun Fact!

This supercarrier runs on nuclear power. With its two nuclear reactors, it never has to stop for gas—it can run for 20 years without refueling!

1

2

3

4

5

6

Did You Know?

The HEMTT provides heavy transport for the supply of combat vehicles and weapons for the US Army.

This eight-wheel diesel truck can carry supplies, fuel tanks, and large artillery.

Mini Quiz

Which of the following is the HEMTT's nickname?
A. Dragon Wagon
B. Green Machine
C. Cargo King
D. All of the above

(Answer on page 64)

1

2

3

4

5

6

Tow Truck

Did You Know?

The tow truck was invented out of necessity in 1916 by Ernest Holmes, Sr. in Tennessee after having to pull a car out of a creek using blocks, ropes, and six men.

This crane-bearing service vehicle has a large cab and plenty of compartments for storing towing tools.

Fun Fact!

Heavy-duty tow trucks can haul loads up to 45,000 pounds; their cargo can include buses, other big trucks, or even buildings!

Mini Quiz Answers

Page 15: True. Its last commercial flight took place in February 2014, but there are cargo versions that continue to operate.

Page 19: C. There are three types of tugboats: seagoing, harbor, and river.

Page 21: D. Commercial planes take about 8 hours to fly from New York to Paris, while the supersonic took about 3.5 hours for transatlantic routes.

Page 31: C. The first ocean steamer credited with crossing the Atlantic ocean was the SS Savannah in 1819.

Page 35: B. Ambulances were first used for emergency transport in 1487 in Spain. The first ambulances date back to ancient times, however, when they were simple carts used to transport sick patients by force.

Page 45: D. Amphibious vehicles are used for different purposes; therefore, some are built on wheels, some on tracks, and even some on air (hovercraft)!

Page 61: A. The HEMTT is also known as the "dragon wagon."